HISTORIC
P&O–ORIENT
LINERS

by
Philip Rentell

For my Mother and Father

© Philip Rentell & Kingfisher Publications
ISBN 0 946184 56 9
1990

Typeset by
PageMerger,
Southampton

Printed by
Conifer Press,
Horndean
Hampshire

INTRODUCTION

The name of P&O is synonymous with world shipping. Dating back to 1839, P&O vessels have plied the world's oceans helping maintain the economies of the many countries on its routes. Over 150 years on, the company retains its importance in the shipment of freight and passengers, although the latter services have clearly altered to the now all important cruise markets.

This book does not pretend to portray a full history of the company or its vessels. It does through the reproduction of many rare colour postcards accomplish a shortened account of some of the company's most famous ships of the past.

In compiling this book I would like to thank the following people and organisations for their invaluable help; to the P&O Group for their help and co-operation and to Stephen Card and Bert Moody for many hours of hard work.

Published by
Kingfisher Publications
65A The Avenue, Southampton SO1 2TA

P. & O. R.M.S. KAISAR-I-HIND, 11,500 TONS GROSS.
India Mail and Passenger Service.

P&O–Orient Line
A BRIEF HISTORY

In 1815 a shipbroking business was opened in London by the Belgium born Englishman, Brodie McGhie Willcox, taking as his clerk a young Scotsman, Arthur Anderson. They acted as voyage brokers for seven years to develop their trade to the Iberian Peninsula. In 1822, they became partners and their firm became known as Willcox and Anderson.

Between 1824 and 1826 they ran a small schooner to carry arms on the side of the Portuguese Royal family during the Civil War there, and on the first voyage Anderson travelled to ensure delivery and payment, sailing under the assumed name of 'Mr Smith'. Normal trade resumed in 1833, although their help was again required during the Spanish uprising. This support for the two Royal houses

brought valuable influence plus the right to fly their Royal Standards. P&O's house flag still has the red and yellow of Spain and the blue and white of Portugal.

In 1835, when the Spanish revolt was at an end, regular steamship services to the Iberian Peninsula were inaugurated by the Dublin and London Steam Packet Co, the firm that Willcox and Anderson had first chartered steamers. Captain Bourne, their owner and James Allen, his partner, came to London and joined the company as part of the agreement whereby Willcox and Anderson would operate the service under the name Peninsular Steam Navigation Co. The first vessel built for the partnership was the *Iberia*, delivered in 1836.

On September 1st 1836, after

being awarded the mail contract, the company announced weekly sailings from London and Falmouth to Vigo, Oporto, Lisbon, Cadiz and Gibraltar. Connections were available to Malta and Corfu, with a monthly connection to Alexandria where it was possible to go overland to Port Suez and then on to India, although at the time this section was not operated by the Peninsular Steam Navigation Co.

INDIA, THE ORIENT AND AUSTRALIA

In 1839, the Governor General of India; Lord William Bentinck proposed a regular service to India, a mail contract was put out to tender by the British Government. Willcox and

2

Anderson secured the contract with a bid of £34,200. Larger ships were required for the service and to increase their capital, the board of the company agreed to change the name of the company to Peninsular and Oriental Steam Navigation Co, which was launched, with a share capital of £1,000,000, by Royal Charter. The company immediately became known as the P&O.

The company divided the route into two halves: west of Egypt and east of Egypt, two new ships being ordered for the latter Suez to Bombay route. On September 24th 1842, the first of these, *Hindostan* left England for the new service. For the next quarter of a century the overland route to India became the quickest way to travel. Passengers had to disembark at Alexandria, travel twelve hours up the Nile to Cosseir, then over the desert by mule-drawn carriage to Suez. The total distance of 250 miles took 88 hours to accomplish.

In 1884 P&O were asked to tender by the Government for the route beyond Ceylon to Penang, Singapore and Hong Kong, and which they were duly awarded. Singapore became the new staging post for the Far East and branch services to Japan and to Australia were considered. Lady Mary Wood inaugurated the new service, arriving in Singapore on August 4th 1845. She also commenced an experimental service between Hong Kong and Shanghai in 1849, the year P&O started its own ship insurance scheme, funded by allocating a percentage of all revenues.

By 1851 a government committee had recommended a service to Australia from Singapore, again P&O's tender was accepted, £119,600 a year for a bi-monthly service. The first ship on the service was the *Chusan* which left Southampton on May 15th 1852, bound for Sydney via the Cape,

P. & O. S.S. VICEROY OF INDIA, 19,700 TONS GROSS.
India Mail and Passenger Service.

Adelaide and Melborne.

The war in Crimea resulted in several of the company's ships being requisitioned, eventually resulting in the suspension of the Australian service. When the war finished in 1856, P&O naturally expected to retain the contract, however, it was awarded to the European & Columbian SN Co for a very low subsidy. In 1857 P&O vessels again saw government service as troopships during the Indian Mutiny. Later that

year, the renamed European and Australian Royal Mail Co ceased trading to Australia having incurred large debts. P&O were awarded the new contract in 1858 for a subsidy of £118,000 per annum and a passage time from England to Australia of 55 days.

It was during this time of hot, steamy passages through the Red Sea, when the humidity, sun and lack of any sort of breeze, the word POSH was said to have been introduced.

R.M.S. STRATHEDEN, P & O LINE
23,722 GROSS TONS   LENGTH 638FT.   SPEED 20 KNOTS   TWIN-SCREW

Naturally, the coolest cabins were away from the sun, port side on the way out and starboard on the way home. Experienced travellers therefore went 'Port Out, Starboard Home'.

FROM THE SUEZ CANAL TO THE GREAT WAR

On November 17th 1869 the Suez Canal opened, P&O's Delta carrying the official guests behind a procession headed by the French Royal Yacht *Aigle*. The opening of the canal, however, was to cause the company some financial embarrassment. Their fleet had been built with the overland connection being a fact of life, freight rates reflecting the trans-shipment costs. Now, not only was the fleet outdated, but all the land and investment tied up with the Egyptian operation became greatly reduced in value. The company was also obliged by contract with the Post Office to send the mail by land across Egypt.

James Allan had taken over the running of the company upon Andersons death in 1868, Wilcox having been killed in 1862. However, Thomas Sutherland, the assistant manager who had opened the Hong Kong Yokohama service in 1864, became a managing director in 1872. He took the bold steps required to rebuild the fleet, eleven new ships being introduced in 1873. In 1874, the mail contracts were renewed, the land trans-shipment clause being dropped, but the subsidy was reduced by £20,000.

Sutherland became chairman in 1881, at the age of 46. In 1883, when the British government were considering a plan to build another canal on British land in Egypt, as a result of French harassment of British ships, he managed to secure places for British interests on the Board of the Suez Canal Co. The plan was therefore dropped.

In January of 1889, P&O introduced an intermediate service to Australia via the Cape, however it proved to be unsuccessful as a result of the competition from the established Union and Castle companies and was withdrawn within a short space of time. The route was not forgotten though and in 1910, the fleet and goodwill of Lund's Blue Anchor Line was acquired. This company, begun in 1896, ran emigrant steamers to Australia via the Cape and was renamed the P&O Branch Line, the service was thereafter maintained until the 1930s.

During the Boer War of 1900-1902, nine P&O liners were taken over by the government as troop ships, transporting over 150,000 personnel.

In early 1914, the Australasian United SN Co was acquired, then in May of that year, British India and

P&O amalgamated. Although a rival, P&O had very close ties with 'BI' many of its routes feeding the P&O mail steamers. The combined fleet was larger than most navies. A joint board of directors consisted of twelve P&O, and eight British India. The British India chairman, James Mackay, later to become the first Lord Inchcape, was to succeed Sutherland as chairman of P&O.

The outbreak of the First World War on August 4th 1914, was to result in almost half the group fleet, 85 vessels of 518,316 tons, being lost. Lord Inchcape put a postwar rebuilding program in hand for 120 vessels.

POST WAR EXPANSION

On 1st July 1916, P&O acquired the New Zealand Shipping Company with its associated Federal Steam Navigation Co. This was followed in August 1917 by the Union Steamship of New Zealand along with the Hain and Norse companies.

The *Naldera*, P&O's first three funnelled liner, came into the fleet in May 1918, her building had commenced in 1913.

Continued growth resulted in a large but minority interest being purchased in the Orient Steam Navigation Co during 1918. This company, established in 1878 by Anderson, Anderson and Green, held the mail contract to Australia via the Cape jointly with P&O from 1888.

British India acquired control of the Eastern & Australasian Mail Co in 1919 and P&O bought out the General Steam Navigation Co in 1920.

In 1923 P&O postponed its rebuilding program as a result of excessive costs, but in that year, the first P&O liner to exceed 20,000 tons, the *Mooltan*, was delivered. In 1924 Lord Inchcape was forced to sell his

investment in the Khedivial Line, bought five years previously.

Viceroy of India, the first large British passenger ship to have turbo-electric propulsion, was delivered in 1929. However P&O were hard hit by the depression of the late 20s and early 30s, no dividend being paid for four years. But the magnificent 'Strath' liners were introduced, *Strathnaver* making her maiden voyage to Australia on October 2nd 1931.

During the Second World War, P&O were to loose 182 ships and the reconstruction program brought new problems. Not only was there strong competition from the newly independent nations and 'flag of convenience' fleets, but the advent of commercial aviation resulted in more and more passengers being able to travel by air. P&O introduced *Chusan* and *Himalaya*, Orient Line, *Oronsay* and *Orcades*, while BI brought out *Uganda* and *Kenya*, and the *Ruahine*, *Rangitane* and *Rangitoto* were built by New Zealand Shipping.

INTO THE CRUISING ERA

1959 saw the introduction of the transpacific service between Australia, and the west coasts of Canada and the United States, it was known as 'Orient and Pacific Line'. The name, however, was unpopular, and was dropped two years later when P&O Orient Lines was formed to manage the two fleets. The largest ship ever to be introduced on the Australian route, *Canberra*, made her maiden voyage in June 1961. The Orient name was finally dropped in 1966, one year after P&O acquired the remaining minority shareholding.

P&O gradually moved more into cruising although regular voyages continued with E&A's run from Australia to the Far East up until 1975. BI's passenger services from

India lasted right up until 1982 when the final service from Bombay to the Gulf finally ceased.

P&O had in fact introduced cruising in 1904. In the 1930s, the BI troopships added educational cruises during the off-season and regularly from 1961 to 1982 with *Dunera*, *Devonia*, *Nevasa* and finally *Uganda*. The present cruising era, however, really began with the introduction of their first purpose-built cruise vessel, *Spirit of London*, in 1973, followed in 1974 by the acquisition of Princess Cruises. This company had its beginnings in 1962, when the industrialist S.T. McDonald chartered the small Canadian vessel *Princess Patricia* to run between California and Seattle. Princess Cruises was then founded in 1965 and used chartered tonnage until the P&O takeover.

The P&O Passenger Division was restyled in 1977 as P&O Cruises Limited. At that time the fleet consisted of *Canberra*, *Pacific Princess*, *Island Princess* and the *Sun Princess*, the ex *Spirit of London*, renamed after the takeover of Princess Cruises. The ex Swedish America liner *Kungsholm* was acquired in 1979 and introduced as the *Sea Princess*. A new, purpose-built vessel, the 45,000 ton *Royal Princess* entered service in 1984. In July 1988, P&O announced the acquisition of the entire share capital of Sitmar Cruises. The Sitmar fleet consisted of four vessels with three new vessels under construction. The acquired ships were renamed *Dawn Princess*, *Fair Princess*, and *Sky Princess*. The *Fairstar* retained her own name and continued operation in the Australian market under the banner of a new division, P&O-Sitmar Cruises. The newest vessel, *Sitmar Fair Majesty*, delivered in 1989, was given the name Star Princess, and a further two vessels, originally ordered by Sitmar, will be delivered to the Princess Cruise Fleet in 1990 and 1991.

Orient
1879-1910

ORIENT-ROYAL MAIL LINE S.S. ORIENT
AT COLOMBO

COMPLETED 1879	PASSENGERS	LENGTH 460 Feet BEAM 46 Feet
GROSS TONNAGE 5,386	220 First Class, 130 Second Class.	300 STEERAGE

Launched from the Glasgow yard of John Elder and Co on June 5 1878, *Orient* was completed with compound engines and capable of 15 knots, being delivered to the Orient Line in September 1879.

She had been built to Admiralty specifications for use as an armed merchant cruiser, but designed for the Australian mail trade, making her maiden voyage from London to Melbourne and Sydney on November 1, the largest ship on the run. Until 1883 she sailed via the Cape of Good Hope outbound and through Suez home. In 1881 refrigeration was fitted and in 1884 she became the first ship on the run to have electric lighting.

In 1895 a serious fire in her coal bunkers, whilst she lay alongside in Melbourne, necessitated her being flooded until she grounded. This may have been the reason why the company decided to give *Orient* a major refit in 1897. Two of her four masts were removed as was one of her two funnels. The old compound engines were replaced with triple expansion reciprocating machinery which increased her speed to 16½ knots. The work was carried out by the Wallsend Slipway Company and she returned to service in June 1898.

The Boer War resulted in *Orient* being used for trooping duties between October 1899 to November 1902, not only voyaging to South Africa, but to New Zealand and even repatriating prisoners from St Helena.

In November 1910 she was finally sold to Luigi Pittaluga Fu Francesca, and towed to the breakers yard at Genoa, being renamed *Oric* for the voyage.

Ophir
1891–1922

ORIENT-ROYAL MAIL LINE S.S. OPHIR
AT CONSTANTINOPLE

COMPLETED 1891	**PASSENGERS**	**LENGTH 465 Feet**
GROSS TONNAGE 6,814	**892 in three classes**	**BEAM 53 Feet**

Handed over by R Napier and Company of Glasgow on 30 October 1891, *Ophir* was the first twin screw ship on the Australian mail service; her triple expansion engines gave a service speed of 18 knots. Sixty five days of arbitration between builders and owners, brought about as a result of her excessive coal consumption (125 tons per day), was settled in favour of the Orient Line.

Between November 1900 and January 1902, *Ophir* was chartered by the Admiralty to convey the Duke and Duchess of York, (later King George V) to Australia where the Duke was to open the first Commonwealth Parliament. As Royal Yacht, she was extensively redecorated and refurnished, the hull being painted white. A round-the-world tour of the Empire followed until the ship resumed commercial sailings.

On the outbreak of the First World War, the British Government converted her to an armed merchant cruiser. Paid off in 1917, she became a hospital ship the following year and served in the Far East.

Ophir was offered for sale by auction in 1920, but the £45,000 bid was not accepted, being below the reserve. Eventually she was sold in 1922 for £6,000 to breakers, who dismantled her at Troon in Scotland.

THE ORIENT-PACIFIC LINE. R.M.S. "OPHIR."

Egypt
1897-1922

P. & O. S.S. "EGYPT" LEAVING MARSEILLES.
(8,000 TONS, 11,000 HORSE-POWER).

COMPLETED 1897	PASSENGERS	LENGTH 500 Feet
GROSS TONNAGE 7,912	314 First Class, 212 Second Class Crew 400	BEAM 54 Feet

The *Egypt* was one of five passenger ships built for P&O's Indian and Australian service. The others were *India*, *China*, *Arabia* and *Persia*. They were all just under 8,000 tons and were powered by triple expansion steam reciprocating machinery. Three single ended and three double ended boilers provided 11,000 indicated horse power to a single propeller, the maximum speed being 16.5 knots. They were the company's largest ships to date.

The *Egypt* was delivered from the yard of Caird and Company at Greenock in August 1897, having cost £239,492. She was to maintain the service to Australia via Bombay until the advent of hostilities in 1914, and brought Her Royal Highness, the Princess Royal, home from Egypt in 1910. During the First World War she was to serve as Hospital Ship number 52, positioned principally in the Mediterranean.

After returning to P&O service when the war finished, she was to survive until 1922. She was unfortunate in having a collision in fog on May 20th of that year with the French ship *Seine* while she was passing the island of Ushant off the north west coast of France. She sank in twenty minutes with the loss of fifteen passengers and seventy one crew. Gold bullion estimated at £1,054,000 also went down with the ship.

By 1935, most of the lost gold had been brought to the surface by the Italian salvage vessel *Artiglio*.

Mongolia
1903-1917

P AND O

s.s. "MONGOLIA."
9,505 Tons.   14,000 h.p.

COMPLETED 1903
Gross tonnage 9,505 tons

PASSENGERS
348 First Class, 166 Second Class
Crew 370

LENGTH 545 Feet
BEAM 58 Feet

Mongolia was the second vessel in a series of ten to enter P&O service. They were the 'M' Class and were unusual in that they increased in size from 9,505 tons to the *Medina* which was 12,358 tons, and completed in 1911. The main machinery was triple expansion steam; three double ended and four single ended boilers gave 12,000 Indicated Horse Power and a service speed of seventeen knots.

Completed by the Greenock yard of Caird & Co, she left for her trials at the end of October, and leaving London for Bombay on her maiden voyage on Friday November 20th, calling at Plymouth, Marseilles, Suez, and Aden. She had been built for the Australian trade and her next voyage was to Sydney. This trip was not without incident; while passing through the Red Sea she was chased by Russian warships. The Russian -

Japanese war had started only twelve days earlier and it was presumed they were looking for an early prize. *Mongolia* was instructed to stop and after doing so a destroyer came close enough to inspect her, then signalled 'Beg to be excused' and allowed *Mongolia* to continue her voyage.

In March of 1908 a fire in one of her holds caused severe damage to cargo and baggage but was extinguished by the Marseilles fire brigade. In December of the same year, while in Freemantle, she collided with the customs tug which unfortunately sank. On June 24th 1911 she took her place along with other passenger ships at the Spithead Coronation Fleet Review.

During the First World War, *Mongolia* continued in service to Australia and she remained unscathed until 1917. In June of that year she left

London on another voyage to Sydney, being escorted all the way to the Suez Canal. After Suez tension decreased and lifeboat drills were frequently carried out. When only seventeen miles from Bombay she struck a mine which had been laid by the German raider *Wolf*. The mine, one of the 'two tier' type, exploded a second time, right under the engine room, killing twenty one engine room staff and passengers. The frequency of the drills was to pay off, as *Mongolia* sank in thirteen minutes, yet no further loss of life was experienced, all of the remaining complement, 450, escaping in the ships boats. The boats made there way under sail to the nearest land where the news was passed to Bombay by telephone. Relief ships were sent out but the passengers had to walk ten miles to Janjira to meet them.

Malwa
1908-1932

P&O. LINER
S.S. MALWA
HORSE POWER 15,000.
TONNAGE 11,500.
LENGTH 558 FEET

COMPLETED 1908	PASSENGERS	LENGTH 540 Feet
GROSS TONNAGE 10,883	400 First Class, 200 Second Class Crew 376	BEAM 61 Feet

M*alwa*, the second P&O vessel to carry this name, was the seventh in the series of ten 'M' class ships built in the 1900s. Like *Mongolia* she was built at Caird's on the Clyde, being launched on October 10th 1908 by the youngest daughter of Patrick Caird, Constance. In just over two months, she sailed on her trials and on January 29th left Tilbury on her maiden voyage, calling at Colombo, Melbourne and Sydney.

Again, P&O installed two sets of compound quadruple expansion machinery, driving twin screws at a maximum speed of eighteen knots.

Upon returning from her maiden voyage she undertook three cruises to the Atlantic Isles, the Norwegian Fjords and a Northern Capitals cruise, as popular then as they are today. In September, she returned to the Australian route, followed in February of 1910 with a call at Auckland, the first P&O liner to visit New Zealand.

Malwa was not initially called upon by the Government when war broke out in 1914, but remained on the somewhat reduced mail service. Until 1917 she survived without incident, however, early in that year she was requisitioned as a troop transport. On May 12th 1917, while sailing in convoy, she narrowly missed a torpedo which passed close under her stern. On November 30th, the conning tower of a submarine was sighted during a voyage through the Irish Sea, in taking evasive action by putting the stern towards the danger, it appears she rammed another submarine; the lookout reported a 'long dark object'. One can only assume the submarines were operating together, the second, in all likelihood, being sunk by *Malwa*.

Her nearest escape, however, was during a trooping voyage in the Mediterranean. On September 22nd 1918, the wake of a torpedo was spotted by the lookouts. Course was adjusted to parallel that of the torpedo, but it glanced off the side, fortunately without exploding, no doubt to everyone's extreme relief.

Malwa returned to P&O shortly after the end of the war, resuming services to India and Australia on September 24th 1920, having first had a major refit. Because only four 'M' Class ships survived the conflict, she was in great demand but as new tonnage entered service she was used on the Far East run to Japan. Her career continued uneventfully and finally in 1932 she was sold to Japanese breakers.

Orsova
1909-1936

R.M.S. ORSOVA.

COMPLETED 1909 GROSS TONNAGE 12,026	PASSENGERS 268 First Class, 120 Second Class, 660 Third Class Crew 350	LENGTH 553 feet BEAM 63 feet

Between the years 1909 to 1911, the Orient Line had six passenger vessels delivered for the trade to Australia, all very much the same with twin funnels and twin masts. In order of delivery, they were *Orsova, Otway, Osterley, Otranto, Orvieto,* and *Orama*. The main machinery was quadruple steam expansion reciprocating engines, four double and two single ended boilers developing 14,000 horse power to twin propellers, giving a service speed of eighteen knots.

Orsova was launched from the John Brown yard on Clydebank on November 7th 1908 and made her maiden voyage from London on June 25th 1909 to Melbourne, Sydney and Brisbane via Suez. All the ships continued in this service until the advent of the First World War, when they were called up as either Auxiliary Cruisers or, as in *Orsova*'s

case, as troop transports, only three were to survive the hostilities.

Otway was a victim of the German submarine UC49 which torpedoed and sank her on July 22nd 1917 while she was passing through the Minches off the west coast of Scotland. She had been a member of the 10th Cruiser squadron. Ten of her complement were killed. *Otranto*, while part of a convoy escort in the Irish Sea, was in collision with the P&O liner *Kashmir* on October 6th 1918. She was run aground off Islay and the destroyer *Mounsey* went to her aid, however, 431 were killed and the ship was lost. The *Orama*, while also acting as an escort, was torpedoed and sunk on October 19th 1917. The submarine, U62, had been patrolling the southern Irish Sea when the seventeen ship

11

convoy was sighted and the *USS Conynham* attempted to ram her unsuccessfully.

Orsova was to have her own adventures, she was torpedoed near the Eddystone lighthouse on March 14th 1917. The damage was severe and six were killed, however, she was successfully beached in Cawsand Bay and later towed into Devonport dockyard for initial repair. This was completed at Liverpool and took until September 1918 when she was again used to carry troops, back to Australia.

She resumed peacetime service for her company in November 1919, returning to the Australia run, which she continued until her withdrawal in 1936. She was broken up in Bo'ness on the Firth of Forth in October of that year. *Osterley* had gone in 1930 and *Orvieto* in 1931.

ORIENT LINE
TO AUSTRALIA

Head Offices—
FENCHURCH AVENUE
LONDON, E.C.

Third Class Cabin

The 'B' Class Ships of 1911 to 1914

This class of five ships were built for the P&O Branch Line to replace those vessels taken over when P&O bought the Blue Anchor Line, which ran services to Australia via South Africa. Until 1914 they carried the Blue Anchor Line colours, a black funnel with a diagonal chained anchor in blue on a white band.

All five ships, named after Australian settlements, were built at the Greenock yard of Caird and Co. They were to carry emigrants in one class, up to 1,100, 850 of which were in accommodation which could be dismantled for the homeward voyage to enable more cargo to be carried.

Main machinery was, as expected, quadruple steam expansion, two double ended and two single ended boilers providing 9,000 Indicated Horse Power to twin screws, giving a service speed of 14 knots.

By March 1914 all five ships, *Ballarat, Beltana, Benalla, Berrima* and *Borda*, were in service, providing a three-weekly service. However, the First World War was soon to intervene, and all were eventually taken up as troop ships. *Benalla* was handed back in January 1915, to enable P&O to carry on some semblance of a service to Australia. This, however, only lasted until later in the year when the Government again used her for transporting troops.

In February 1917 the *Berrima* was torpedoed off Portland Bill, killing four men. The crew abandoned her as the water rose in the engine room. However, as the next dawn appeared she still had not sunk, some of her men going back aboard to attach a line to a tug. She was slowly towed into Portland harbour where the salvage pumps were put to work and she

eventually returned to her duties.

On April 25th 1917, *Ballarat*, with 1,400 Australian troops, was twenty five miles from the Scilly Isles when she was struck by a torpedo fired by the German submarine U-32. She started sinking by the stern and all the ships company were ordered to abandon ship, some being taken off by *HMS Lookout*. There was no loss of life, which must speak volumes as to the courage and discipline of everyone on board.

All four remaining ships survived the war to continue in commercial service for their owner in early 1920.

The following year *Benalla* was involved in a collision with the tanker *Patella* in the English Channel.

Number four hold was flooded and it was thought advisable to beach her in Pevensey Bay. *Benalla* was refloated and also returned to London where she was repaired.

A second series of Branch Line steamers joined the fleet after the war, the remaining original four getting long in the tooth by the late twenties. The trade had started to decline so, in March 1930 the first, *Beltana*, was sold to a Japanese company who intended to use her in the whaling trade - this fell through however, and she was eventually broken up in 1933. By the end of 1930 all had been sold, the last, *Benalla*, going to Japanese breakers the following January.

GROSS TONNAGE 11,100 BUILT BETWEEN 1911 and 1914	PASSENGERS 1,100 One Class.	LENGTH 500 Feet BEAM 62 Feet

13

Kaisar - I - Hind
1914-1938

P. & O.S.S. "KAISAR-I-HIND."
(11,518 TONS, 16,000 HORSE-POWER.)

COMPLETED 1914 GROSS TONNAGE 11,430	PASSENGERS 315 First Class, 333 Second Class Crew 367	LENGTH 520 Feet BEAM 61 Feet

Built by Caird & Co of Greenock, *Kaisar - I - Hind* was the second P&O liner to bear the name, which means 'Empress of India'. Launched on June 28th 1914, she cost £363,176, and was rapidly fitted out as a result of the Great War. She left Tilbury on the River Thames on October 24th for Bombay, setting a new record of just under eighteen days.

The *Kaisar*'s propulsion machinery was two inverted quadruple expansion engines which drove twin screws at a maximum speed of 18.5 knots. Four double ended and four single ended boilers provided 14,000 Indicated Horse Power.

During 1916, her Bombay service was extended to Australia. Then the following year, the Government acquired the *Kaisar* for trooping

duties, mainly in the Mediterranean. It was during this period that she had her luckiest escape. On April 22nd 1918, while carrying 3,000 troops, she was hit in the vicinity of the engine room by a torpedo which failed to explode. When drydocked, the hull plates which had been dented were painted a bright green, in contrast to her normal red boot topping and remained so for several years until they were eventually replaced. From then on she was known as 'Lucky Kaisar'.

When the war finished she was still employed in Government service, repatriating troops to Australia and also British troops to India, finally being handed back to P&O in 1920. During 1921 the *Kaisar* was chartered by Cunard Line for one Atlantic voyage, being renamed *Emperor of*

India. During the returning cruise, via Scandinavia, there was a stokehold explosion which killed three Indian firemen.

After a long overhaul she re-entered P&O service to Bombay in October 1921, remaining in this trade for her remaining career, although after 1929 she also continued to the Far East. During a regular call at Malta, in November 1931, her anchor dragged and she collided with the Italian ship *Citta Di Trieste*, sinking a few wooden lighters in the process.

With the introduction of new vessels and the company's refusal to re-engine her, the *Kaisar* made her final voyage to Japan from Tilbury on January 14th 1938.

Ormonde
1918-1952

ORIENT LINE TO AUSTRALIA.
S.S. "ORMONDE," TWIN SCREW, 14,853 TONS.

COMPLETED 1918
Gross Tons 14,853

PASSENGERS
278 First Class, 195 Second Class,
1,000 Third Class. Crew 380

Length 600 feet. Beam 67 Feet

Ormonde was actually laid down in May of 1913, but building at John Brown's Clydebank yard was delayed by the advent of hostilities, and she was not launched until February 1917. It had been decided to complete her as a troopship and in June 1918 she went into Government service. Ormonde was a turbine steamer, the Orient Line being more willing to experiment with this relatively new means of propulsion than the P&O. She had four double and two single ended boilers providing steam to four geared turbines, driving twin screws at eighteen knots.

Completing her Government service the following year, she made her maiden commercial voyage on November 15th from London to Australia, the trade for which she had originally been intended. Her boilers were converted in 1923 from coal to oil burning, which no doubt pleased not only her engineers, but also her Chief Officer whose responsibility it was to maintain the whiteness of her decks. In 1933 she was converted to one class, with a capacity of 777 tourist class, but remained on the Australia run until being requisitioned yet again in 1939. She became a troopship and during the Second World War saw action in several arenas.

She was to take part in the troop evacuations of France and Norway and, in 1942, proceeded to the Mediterranean theatre to be present during the landings at North Africa, Sicily and Italy. In 1944 she went to Bombay to be based in that port for Far East trooping duties. Finally, in April 1947, she was handed back and sent to the Cammell Laird yard at Liverpool to be refitted as an emigrant ship. Her tonnage increased to 15,047 as a result and her capacity became 1,070 third class passengers. Her first voyage in this new guise was on October 10th from London to Melbourne.

Eventually she completed her last voyage in December 1952 and went to breakers at Dalmuir in Scotland, her career having spanned a respectable thirty four years.

Ormuz
1920-1927 (1934)

ORIENT LINE—S.S. ORMUZ, 14,167 TONS REGISTER.

COMPLETED 1915	PASSENGERS	LENGTH 570 Feet
GROSS TONNAGE 14,167	293 First Class, 882 Third Class Crew 320	BEAM 67 Feet

The second Ormuz was in fact launched from Bremer Vulkan Vegesack at Bremen in Germany on June 9th 1914 as Norddeutscher Lloyd's *Zeppelin* and completed the following January but laid up for the duration of the First World War. She was a quadruple expansion steamer with twin screws, capable of sixteen knots and had originally been designed for the North Atlantic trade, with emphasis on the carriage of emigrants to America, her original passenger capacity being in excess of 2,500.

After the war she was handed over to the British Government as reparations and first managed for the shipping controller by White Star Line. Orient Line bought her in 1920 and she was renamed *Ormuz*. After a considerable refit at Belfast and Rotterdam she made her first voyage from London to Australia on November 12th 1921.

Ormuz remained with Orient only until 1927 when she returned to North German Lloyd, who put her into service on the Bremerhaven to New York run. On June 29th 1934, *Ormuz* ran aground near the Norwegian island of Utsire during a cruise. She had been badly holed and beached as a precaution on Karmoy Island. The passengers were transferred safely to the shore. The next day she took on a list and capsized, becoming a total constructive loss, four of the ships complement being killed. The wreck was later broken up by a Stavanger firm.

Naldera
1920-1938

Naldera and Narkunda were ordered by the outgoing P&O chairman, Sir Thomas Sutherland, prior to the First World War, Naldera in November 1913 from the Greenock yard of Caird and Co. Work on both ships was suspended for the first three years of the war, however, in 1917, it was decided to bring them to a condition suitable for launch, as the slips were urgently required for more pressing needs. Naldera was launched on December 29th, her fate undecided by the Government, although she was actually completed as a troopship in May 1918. However, it was then anticipated she might become a hospital ship or possibly an aircraft carrier! Fortunately the war ended and she was handed back to her owners who refitted her to her intended role for the Australian trade, finally entering service on March 24th 1920 and making her maiden voyage to Sydney on April 10th.

In line with company policy both ships were fitted with quadruple expansion steam machinery, driving twin screws. A service speed of 17.5 knots, maximum 18.5 knots, was obtained from four double ended and two single ended boilers which developed 18,000 horse power.

When leaving Bombay on July 29th 1921, she had a collision with the Clan Lamont, a British cargo ship at anchor and, although there were no injuries, she had to put back into port to repair damage to her bow. She had another collision, this time at Tilbury in 1924 during docking, when the Scotstoun Head, a coastal cargo vessel, hit her port side. Damage was light

however, and she sailed again for Bombay two weeks later.

Naldera's voyages were advertised by the travel agents Thomas Cook as 'round the world voyages', the fare being £1,400 per person.

Naldera had other adventures during her career. In July 1930, during a storm in the Pacific, water was taken into number two hold causing damage to the meat cargo, hundreds of tons of which had to be jettisoned. In October 1934 she ran aground in the Suez Canal during a southbound transit and took twenty four hours to refloat, after some of her cargo was discharged. Then, in January 1937, she damaged her starboard propeller whilst docking at Southampton.

When new ships were brought in for the Australian service in 1931, Naldera was transferred to the London,

Bombay and Far East service. Unlike her sister she was not converted to oil fuel which was probably a factor the company considered when deciding to take her out of service in 1938. Her final passenger sailing from London, to Kobe, Japan, was on May 20th arriving back on September 23rd. She had a brief reprieve when it was decided to use her to carry the 'British Legion Volunteer Police'. This body of men were to supervise the voting in Czechoslovakia over Hitler's partition, however their services were not required after a decision was made to appease Hitler during this period of political confrontation. The men who had embarked were stood down and Naldera was sold for £36,000 to McClellan of Glasgow. On November 19th she left Tilbury for the breakers at Bo'ness in the Firth of Forth.

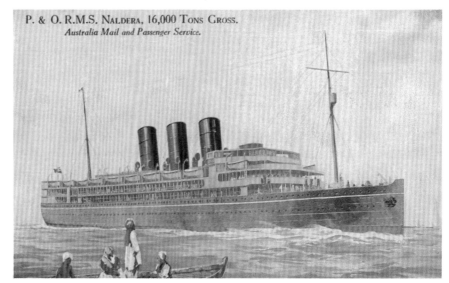

P. & O. R.M.S. NALDERA, 16,000 Tons Gross.
Australia Mail and Passenger Service.

COMPLETED 1920 GROSS TONNAGE 16,088	PASSENGERS 426 First Class, 247 Second Class Crew 462	LENGTH 600 Feet BEAM 67 Feet

Narkunda
1920-1942

The *Narkunda*, sister ship to *Naldera*, was ordered from the Belfast yard of Harland & Wolff and laid down in 1914. However, the Great War intervened and, like her sister, *Narkunda* remained on the stocks unattended until 1917 when work resumed, primarily to clear the slip for more urgent work. She was launched on April 25th, 1918. The Government, who had taken over the incomplete hull, could not come to a decision as to whether she should be completed as a troop ship, hospital ship, armed merchant cruiser or even an aircraft carrier. Fortunately the end of the war came and the hull was handed back to P&O who completed her on March 30th 1920, a week after her sister. On April 24th she left London on her maiden voyage to Bombay.

The two vessels were the first P&O ships to have three funnels and cruiser sterns, the *Narkunda* differing from her sister by the inclusion of a short forecastle.

After returning from Bombay, *Narkunda* left London on July 9th for Sydney and the Australian run, for which she had been designed, being P&O's largest ship. She had a capacity for 8,700 tons of cargo carried in six hatches, much of the space being insulated.

The company had remained faithful to steam expansion machinery, believing it to be more reliable on the longer runs, the two sisters were no exception and *Narkunda* had twin screws driven by two quadruple-expansion engines capable of developing 18,000 indicated horse power and a speed of 18.5 knots,

although the normal service speed was 17.5 knots. The third funnel was a dummy, balancing the profile.

She became a favourite on the Australia run and remained there even when *Naldera* had been transferred to the Far East route upon the advent of the 'big white ships', *Strathnaver* and *Strathaird*. In 1927 *Narkunda* was converted to burn oil fuel and her second class accommodation was later upgraded and renamed the more acceptable title of tourist class. By 1939 the company had intended to withdraw *Narkunda* and send her to the breakers. Her life was extended, however, by the advent of the Second World War. She made her last commercial sailing to Sydney on June 23rd 1939. Whilst in Colombo there was an explosion in number six hatch, which killed four crew members and injured a further twenty three.

Before trooping, a journey to Lourenco Marques in Mozambique was made during the summer of 1942 to pick up British diplomats in exchange for Japanese diplomats held by the allies. The trip was unusual in that four large Union Jacks and the word 'Diplomats' was painted on the ships side.

On November 1st 1942, *Narkunda* left the UK for the last time, carrying troops for the invasion of North Africa. On November 13th she was struck by a torpedo fired by the Italian submarine *Platino*. She survived the attack sufficiently to make it into Bougie, Algeria, where the troops were disembarked. She left the next day but was attacked by German aircraft and sank with the loss of thirty one lives.

P. & O. INDIA-CHINA-AUSTRALIA MAIL AND PASSENGER SERVICES.

S.S. "NARKUNDA" { 16,000 TONS. 20,000 H.P.

COMPLETED 1920
GROSS TONNAGE 16,118

PASSENGERS
426 First Class, 247 Second Class
Crew 462

LENGTH 605 Feet
BEAM 70 Feet

Moldavia
1922-1938

P. & O. R.M.S. MOLDAVIA, 16,500 TONS GROSS.
Australia Mail and Passenger Service.

4 months tour to Australia & New Zealand 28 Dec 1934 to May 1935 [handwritten]

COMPLETED 1922
GROSS TONNAGE 16,436

PASSENGERS
222 First Class, 175 Second Class.
Crew 337

LENGTH 552 Feet
BEAM 72 Feet

The *Moldavia*, the second to carry the name, was the first P&O liner to have steam turbines. They were double reduction geared to twin screws, fed by three double ended and four single ended boilers, giving an indicated horse power of 13,250, and a service speed of sixteen knots. This was increased to seventeen knots, however, in 1934 when steam superheaters were added, together with new propellers.

Built by Cammell Laird & Co of Birkenhead, she was launched on October 1st 1921 and completed the following September. After acceptance by her owners she commenced loading at Tilbury on the Thames and sailed on her maiden voyage on October 13th bound for Bombay and Sydney. Although the largest company vessel

on that trade to date, her passenger capacity was less than that of *Naldera* and *Narkunda*, although she had more cargo capacity.

Over the next seven years only one incident is recorded, a fire which broke out in number three hold prior to sailing from Fremantle on December 26th 1923. Fibre loaded in Colombo ignited and was extinguished with help from the local fire brigade, causing a great deal of damage to both the cargo and passengers hold baggage.

During her refit of 1928, her boilers were converted from coal firing to oil, her second class accommodation was redesignated third, and a second funnel was added. This, of course, was a dummy put on to balance her profile and stem previous criticism levelled at her appearance

since her building. Unfortunately it was placed too far aft and completely unbalanced her looks. By August of 1931 her accommodation was changed again, this time to all one class, 'tourist', with a capacity for 830 passengers.

Moldavia's final years were spent not only in the Australian trade, but also cruising. She used to carry British tourists during the summer months to ports in the Mediterranean, Europe and the Atlantic Isles. But after only fifteen years of service, she was to make her final voyage in 1937. Leaving London on September 17th for Sydney, she returned on Christmas Eve, only to be laid up for four months at Tilbury. Eventually she was bought on April 18th of the following year by John Cashmore Ltd, who dismantled her.

19

Forward dining saloon on the *Moldavia*.

Moldavia's lounge.

Mooltan & Maloja
1923-1954

COMPLETED 1923
GROSS TONNAGE 20,840

PASSENGERS
327 First Class, 329 Second Class
Crew 422

LENGTH 600 Feet
BEAM 73 Feet

The sister ships *Mooltan* and *Maloja* were the first of the company vessels to exceed 20,000 tons and the largest capable of passing through the Suez Canal. Part of the post war rebuilding programme, they were built in Belfast at the Harland and Wolff yard, and P&O returned to traditional steam reciprocating machinery, both being quadruple expansion, twin screw vessels of 16,000 horse power and capable of sixteen knots.

Mooltan was the first, being launched on February 15th 1923, completed in September and leaving Tilbury on her maiden voyage to Bombay on October 5th. *Maloja* followed her off the stocks on April

P. & O. INDIA-CHINA-AUSTRALIA MAIL AND PASSENGER SERVICES.
S.S. MOOLTAN. { 21,000 TONS.
{ 15,300 H.P.

19th and commenced her maiden voyage on November 2nd. Following the normal practice of initial voyages to India, both vessels were placed on the Australia run which they maintained until the advent of the Second World War. They were fitted in 1929 with auxiliary low pressure turbo-electric machinery, which increased their speed to seventeen knots.

The two liners were converted in 1939 to armed merchant cruisers, armed with eight 6 inch guns and two 3 inch aircraft guns. The after funnel, which was a dummy, had to be removed to improve the arc of fire, but later, shortened versions were replaced to help the engine room ventilation. *Mooltan* was based at Freetown in Sierra Leone, *Maloja*, however, was allocated the Faroes Iceland gap, first seeing action on March 12th 1940 when she stopped the German cargo

vessel *La Coruna*, the crew of which set her on fire then scuttled her. *Maloja* picked up the crew then sunk her with gunfire. She was to join *Mooltan* on the South Atlantic station in June of that year. *Mooltan* was also to see action. During a southbound voyage to Freetown she was attacked by German aircraft, suffering several near misses which caused sufficient damage for her to turn back for repairs.

In 1941 it was decided to convert both vessels to carry troops and they were used for this purpose during the North Africa landings of 1942. Even when the war was over, they were retained in Government service carrying troops to Bombay and Colombo and later used to bring home prisoners of war and civilian internees after the Japanese surrender.

Finally, in 1947, the Government returned them both to P&O. *Mooltan* was refitted by her builders, while

Maloja went to R.&H. Green and Silley Weir at Tilbury. The original second funnels were replaced, but the after mast wasn't, while the buff painted superstructure was carried further down onto the hull making them look far less 'heavy'. Passenger capacity was increased to 1,030 tourist class to take advantage of the Australian Government assisted passage scheme. *Mooltan*'s passengers were to suffer an outbreak of smallpox during April 1949 and six people died.

Eventually the immigrant trade diminshed and on January 7th 1954 *Mooltan* returned from her last voyage. She was sold to the British Iron and Steel Corporation and left Tilbury on the 20th to be broken up at Faslane. *Maloja* was to follow soon after, arriving back from Australia on February 19th and delivered to Inverkeithing on April 2nd.

Mongolia
1923-1938 (1965)

P&O's third *Mongolia* was a product of the Tyne yard of Armstrong Whitwoth, being launched on 24th August 1922 by Miss Elsie Mackay, youngest daughter of the chairman Lord Inchcape. Similar in appearance to *Moldavia*, she was also built for the Australian immigrant trade and had double reduction geared turbines which gave her a speed of sixteen knots.

Trials were conducted on April 26th of the following year, after which she proceeded to Tilbury, making her maiden departure on May 11th for Sydney. She was converted to oil burning in 1928 and in early 1931, as a result of the diminishing numbers of emigrants to Australia, her accommodation was converted to 'tourist', her capacity being increased to 840.

Over the years she was to suffer a number of minor incidents. In 1938 she lost an anchor when entering Copenhagen, resulting in a collision with the *British Venture*, a small tanker, then hitting the breakwater and running aground. There was little damage, however, and she was soon refloated. In December 1936, while in Marseilles, high winds caused her to come in contact with *Villa de Madrid*, a Spanish cargo ship, again there were no injuries and little damage. However, on November 27th 1937 she collided with the collier *Corfleet* in the Thames, suffering considerable bow damage. It was to be her last voyage under the P&O flag and she was laid up at Tilbury.

Unlike her near sister, *Moldavia*, she was to allude the breakers torch for some considerable time. In May 1938 she was chartered to the New Zealand

Shipping Company and renamed *Rimutaka*, being placed on the London to Wellington route. On the advent of the Second World War she was requisitioned by the Government, but generally remained on the New Zealand route via Panama, surviving the hostilities without misfortune. She was to remain with NZS until 1950 when she was sold to the Incres Line and renamed *Europa*. For fifteen months *Europa* was to run between Antwerp and New York, but this was obviously not a success for, in October 1951, she was converted in Genoa, renamed *Nassau* and employed cruising in the Caribbean.

Even this disguise was not to be her final one, she was sold again in 1961 to the Mexican company Natumex. She was to undergo an extensive refit in Fairfields Clyde yard, which altered her profile by extending her superstructure and tapering her funnel and came out with the name *Acapulco*. An initial cruise out of New York was cancelled as a result of the US Coast Guard reporting her as being below required safety standards. The following year she was to be used as a floating hotel, remaining alongside at Seattle during the World's Fair. By May 1963 she had come to the end of her cruising days and was laid up in the small Mexican port of Manzanillo where she remained for eighteen months, eventually being sold to Japanese breakers and arriving at Osaka in December 1964.

Her career had spanned forty one years, a considerable achievement for a large passenger vessel, particularly as she had been only a moderate success for her original owners.

P. & O. INDIA-CHINA-AUSTRALIA MAIL AND PASSENGER SERVICES.
S.S. "MONGOLIA" | 16,000 TONS. 13,000 H.P.

COMPLETED 1923
GROSS TONNAGE 16,385

LENGTH 552 Feet
BEAM 72 Feet

PASSENGERS
230 First Class, 180 Second Class
Crew 337

Ranpura
1925-1944 (1961)

P. & O. S.S. RANPURA, 16,600 TONS GROSS.
India Mail and Passenger Service.

COMPLETED 1925
GROSS TONNAGE 16,585

PASSENGERS
310 First Class, 282 Second Class
Crew 357

LENGTH 570 Feet
BEAM 71 Feet

The *Ranpura* was the first of four post war liners completed for the Indian run, the others being *Ranchi*, *Rawalpindi* and *Rajputana*. Launched on September 13th 1924, *Ranpura* came from the Tyne yard of Hawthorn Leslie and fitted with twin screws propelled by the ever reliable quadruple expansion steam reciprocating machinery. The six double ended boilers gave an indicated horse power of 15,000 and a speed of seventeen knots.

Delivered in April of the following year, she went straight onto the Tilbury - Bombay service, later made one trip to Australia in 1929, and then placed on the Far East route to Japan and China along with the other three in the early 'thirties. On 6th April 1936, *Ranpura* went aground during a fierce gale as she approached Gibraltar. She was carrying Chinese art treasures back to the Far East, and such was the importance of the cargo that a Navy destroyer was escorting her, fortunately she was refloated and no damage found.

Prior to the Second World War, hostilities had developed between Japan and China, and in May 1939, *Ranpura* was stopped by a Japanese cruiser four miles outside Hong Kong, blank shots being fired. The British destroyer *Duchess* came to her aid and protests were made. In August of that year, when war was declared, she had arrived in Aden and was then sent to Calcutta where she was converted to an armed merchant cruiser, the after dummy funnel being removed to make a better firing arc for her anti-aircraft guns. Initially *Ranpura* was based at Port Said then moved to Halifax, Nova Scotia, and finally in August 1942 to the East Indies.

She arrived back on the Clyde just before Christmas 1943 and it was then that the Admiralty decided to purchase her outright and convert her to a heavy repair ship. The work took place in Portsmouth and took over two years. Although initially it was intended to base her in the Far East, she only got as far as Malta, where she remained with the British Mediterranean fleet until early 1947 when she returned to the UK to be based at Rosyth. She was to take part in the Suez crisis in 1956, then, in May of 1958, she went into the reserve fleet at Devonport. Finally she was sold to shipbreakers at La Spezia, arriving there in May 1961.

23

Cathay
1925-1942

COMPLETED 1925
GROSS TONNAGE 15,104

PASSENGERS
203 First Class, 103 Second Class
Crew 278

LENGTH 547 Feet
BEAM 70 Feet

Cathay was the first of three medium sized passenger ships built for the Australian trade, the others being *Comorin* and *Chitral*. Built by Barcaly Curle & Co Ltd at Glasgow, *Cathay* was launched on October 31st 1924. Again P&O decided to install steam expansion machinery which gave a speed of sixteen knots, three double ended and four single ended boilers giving 13,000 IHP.

The maiden voyage from Tilbury commenced on March 27th 1925, and ports of call were Marseilles, Suez, Aden, Colombo, Fremantle, Sydney and Brisbane. Bombay was added to the route in 1932. On December 15th 1933, whilst on passage to Fremantle, *Cathay* lost her port propeller. She

continued her voyage safely on the remaining one.

At the start of the Second World War *Cathay*, like other P&O vessels, was converted to an armed merchant cruiser. She had been on an outward voyage which was terminated at Bombay where the conversion took place. For the first year of hostilities she was based in the Indian Ocean between Bombay and Durban. From January until September 1941 she was to be used on escort duties in the North Atlantic followed by a conversion to troopship at the Brooklyn yard of Bethlehem Steel.

Her new roll commenced in May 1942 and she carried troops to South Africa, Egypt and India. On October 26th she left the Clyde with troops

bound for North Africa as part of Operation 'Torch'. Some troops were landed at Algiers where German aircraft attacked. She proceeded to Bougie where the remaining troops disembarked, again aircraft attacked during the afternoon. Around 1700hrs she received several direct hits and a stick of bombs exploded close to the ships side near the engine room. These caused sufficient damage to warrant the ship being abandoned. Later that night a delayed action bomb exploded, the ship caught fire and the blaze raged all night. At 0700hrs the following morning the fire caused an ammunition stowage to explode, blowing off her stern and causing her to sink three hours later.

Orontes
1929-1962

The Orient Line was to order five passenger vessels for delivery in the mid-1920s. The first was the *Orama* in 1924, followed by *Oronsay*, *Otranto*, *Orford* and finally *Orontes* in 1929. They were built by Vickers-Armstrong at Barrow in Furness for the Australian trade and were all twin screw, steam turbine vessels capable of twenty knots.

Orontes was launched on February 26th 1929 and completed the following July. Her first few initial voyages were cruises out of the UK. The maiden voyage to Australia commenced on October 26th, joining her four other sisters to compete with the P&O on this most lucrative of trades for which her large tourist accommodation was most suited.

The ships maintained this route until the advent of the Second World War, when they were all requisitioned by the Government and converted for trooping duties. *Orontes* and *Otranto* were the only two to survive the conflict. The *Orama*, part of the North Sea convoy which included *HMS Glorious* and three other units, was caught by the German High Seas fleet comprising of *Scharnhorst*, *Gneisenau* and *Admiral Hipper*, three hundred miles off Narvik and all were sunk. *Orford* was also lost in 1940. She was bombed while at anchor off Marseilles during the evacuation of British troops. Fourteen were killed and the ship was beached. She lay there until 1947 when she was refloated and towed away to Italy to be scrapped. *Oronsay* lasted until 1942 when she was torpedoed about 400 miles west of

Monrovia in West Africa. She had not been carrying troops and the majority of the crew were rescued, only five being lost.

When *Otranto* was returned to The Orient Line she was converted to a one class ship, having berths for over 1,400 immigrants in 'tourist' class, the trade which she maintained until her demise in 1957.

Orontes had been present at the North African landings in 1942, the Sicilian landings at Avola in 1943 and later the Italian landings in Salerno. In 1945 she was in Far East waters prior to the invasion of Japan. She was

released from Government service in 1947 and underwent a large refit at J.I. Thornycroft in Southampton Docks, making her return to the Australian trade on June 17th 1948. In 1953, after the old *Ormonde* had gone, she was converted to one class, being employed in the 'tourist' trade along with the *Otranto*.

She reached the ripe old age of thirty three before P&O - Orient Line decided to take her out of service. In March 1962 she completed her last voyage to the breakers yard at Valencia in Spain.

COMPLETED 1929
GROSS TONNAGE 19,970

PASSENGERS
500 First Class, 1,112 Third Class
Crew 420

LENGTH 664 Feet
BEAM 75 Feet

Viceroy of India
1929-1942

P. & O. S.S. VICEROY OF INDIA, 19,700 TONS GROSS.
India Mail and Passenger Service.

COMPLETED 1929
GROSS TONNAGE 19,648

PASSENGERS
415 First Class, 258 Second Class
Crew 417

LENGTH 612 Feet
BEAM 76 Feet

The *Viceroy of India* was probably the most outstanding P&O ship built between the two wars. She was the first of their turbo-electric powered vessels and her accommodation matched some of the great Atlantic liners. There was even a replica of an old baronial hall complete with fireplace, suit of armour and effects of Bonnie Prince Charlie.

When ordered in April of 1927, it had been intended to name her *Taj Mahal*, however, this was changed prior to the launch on 15th September 1928. She was in fact launched by the wife of the Viceroy, Lady Irwin, from

P. & O. S.S. VICEROY OF INDIA, 19,700 TONS GROSS.
India Mail and Passenger Service.

the Glasgow yard of Alexander Stephen & Sons. Unlike other P&O liners of the time, she was assigned for both the direct India service and for cruising. Her steam turbines were built by Stephen's, but her electric motors came from British Thomson-Houston of Rugby, her six boilers providing 17,000 horse power, giving a service speed of nineteen knots from her twin screws.

The maiden voyage commenced on March 29th 1929 to Bombay from London, and was followed by cruising out of the UK. In 1932 she broke the London to Bombay record in a time of just over sixteen days. In September 1935 she was to rescue passengers from the unfortunate White Star vessel *Doric*, which had been in collision off the Portuguese coast. 241 were taken

by the *Viceroy*, the remainder, over 400, went to the Orient Lines *Orion*, which also answered the distress call.

On April 11th 1937, *Viceroy* went aground in the Suez Canal on a homeward voyage. She was not refloated until late that night, and it was found that the rudder had sustained some damage, fortunately not enough to prevent the remainder of her voyage. Repairs were effected at Tilbury.

When the Second World War was declared she abandoned her cruising season and was placed on the Far East route via Suez. On her last passenger voyage, via the Cape in August 1940, she took on passengers from Shaw Savill's *Ceramic* which had been in collision with the *Testbank*. On her return to the UK, she was converted to

a troopship at Liverpool and made several voyages in this role.

She left the Clyde in October 1942 bound for North Africa with troops taking part in 'Operation Torch'. They were disembarked safely on November 7th. Three days later she left bound for home and was unfortunate enough to meet the U407, which was recharging batteries on the surface. A torpedo was fired which struck her amidships, killing four in the engine room. The remaining complement of 451 abandoned ship and were rescued by the destroyer *HMS Boadicea*. Just after 0800hrs on November 11th, *Viceroy of India* sunk, thirty four miles from the North African port of Oran.

Carthage
1931-1961

P. & O. R.M.S. CARTHAGE, 15,000 TONS GROSS.
India and Far Eastern Mail Service.

COMPLETED 1931 GROSS TONNAGE 14,304	PASSENGERS 175 First Class, 196 Second Class Crew 279	LENGTH 522 Feet BEAM 71 Feet

Carthage and her sister *Corfu* were built by Alexander Stephen on the Clyde. They were built to replace the 'N' class on the Far East run and were fitted with steam turbines, 14,000 IHP giving them a service speed of eighteen knots. *Carthage* was launched on August 18th 1931 and completed on November 28th. Her first voyage took her to Japan and China, arriving in Shanghai on February 14th, a city under seige by the Japanese, who were intent on taking over. At one stage shells landed close by the ship but she escaped undamaged. There followed one voyage to Australia, but she was to return to her intended route.

When war was declared in 1939, *Carthage* was in Hong Kong. She was to proceed to Colombo then Calcutta for conversion to an armed merchant cruiser, being commissioned on December 29th 1939 with her second dummy funnel removed. She was based in the Indian Ocean on convoy duties. During this period she was to be part of the British force which intercepted a Vichy French convoy. The *Cap Padaran*, which had been sabotaged by her crew, was taken under tow to Port Elizabeth in South Africa.

In the middle of 1943 it was decided to convert her to a troopship, and she proceeded to Norfolk, Virginia, for the work to be completed, then being based at Calcutta. Finally, when the war was over, she was handed back to her owners and she returned to her builders to be refitted to her original role. The original P&O black colour scheme was dropped and she was painted all white, her single funnel remaining, but lengthened and painted buff, a very elegant livery.

Carthage returned to the Far East run in July 1948, her terminal port now being Hong Kong. Along with

28

Corfu, this service was maintained for the next twelve years, only being varied by the Suez crisis in 1956, which entailed her routing via the Cape. After thirty years of commendable service she was withdrawn from service on February 13th 1961. On the 26th she left Tilbury as the *Carthage Maru*, having been bought by Japanese shipbreakers, arriving at Osaka in May.

Above: First class dining saloon.

Left: First class saloon lounge.

Below: First class saloon smoking room.

Strathnaver
1931-1962

COMPLETED 1931 GROSS TONNAGE 22,547	PASSENGERS 498 First Class, 670 Tourist Class Crew 500	LENGTH 639 Feet BEAM 80 Feet

In 1929 the order for two 21 knot liners for the Australian trade went to Vickers Armstrong of Barrow in Furness, they were to be known as *Strathnaver* and *Strathaird* and were the forerunners of many P&O vessels to come. For the machinery the company returned to turbo-electric, four boilers and two 750 kilowatt turbo alternators providing 28,000 IHP to twin screws and a maximum speed of 23 knots being obtainable. *Strathnaver* was the first to be launched on February 5th 1931 and she commenced her maiden voyage on October 2nd. The two ships were painted white with buff funnels, a departure from the normal colour scheme and one which has been maintained ever since. Along with some cruising from the UK, she was to maintain the Australian run until the advent of the Second World War.

When war was declared she was in Australian waters. The vessel was painted grey and one six inch and one three inch gun were positioned on the poop, (they had been carried on board in crates for such an eventuality). She returned to Liverpool to be converted to a troopship along with her sister.

She was to travel the world in her new guise and was to have some close escapes. During the North African landings of 1942, torpedo, mine and bomb attacks were made by the enemy, yet she remained unscathed. She was used in the Red Sea as a training ship for the invasion of Italy and followed the allies as they proceeded up into Italian waters.

Even after the war had finished, *Strathnaver* was to remain in Government service, repatriating Commonwealth troops, finally being released in November 1948. She was

reconditioned at the Belfast yard of Harland & Wolff, the forward and after dummy funnels being removed. Her first commercial voyage was from Tilbury on January 5th 1950, both ships resuming the trade to Australia. The Government was to charter *Strathnaver* again, this time for the Coronation Review at Spithead on June 15th 1953, when she was used to take official guests to view the fleet.

In 1954 both ships were converted to one class, being able to carry 1,252 'tourists'. Eventually, with both ships thirty years old, P&O took the decision to withdraw them from service. *Strathaird* was the first to go in June 1961 followed by *Strathnaver* in March of the following year. They were both sold to the Shun Fung Ironworks and broken up in Hong Kong.

P. & O. Electric Ship STRATHNAVER, 22,500 Tons.
Carrying First-class and Tourist-class Passengers.
India and Australia Mail Service.

P. & O. 'STRATHAIRD' B DECK SMOKING ROOM

Strathmore
1935-1963 (1969)

P. & O. R.M.S. STRATHMORE, 23,500 TONS.
Carrying First-class and Tourist-class Passengers
India and Australia Mail Service.

COMPLETED 1935 GROSS TONNAGE 23,580	PASSENGERS 445 First Class, 665 Second Class Crew 515	LENGTH 665 Feet BEAM 82 Feet

Strathmore was to be the third 'white strath' to be built for the Australian trade. Again, Vickers at Barrow in Furness were to be the builders and she was launched by the Duchess of York, now Her Majesty the Queen Mother, on Thursday April 4th 1935. Completed the following September, her maiden voyage, a shakedown cruise to the Atlantic Isles and the Iberian Penninsular, commenced on September 27th.

In appearance the most notable difference between her and her predecessors, was a single stack instead of three. Down below, a geared reduction steam turbine plant was installed rather than turbo-electric. The service speed was twenty knots, six boilers developing 24,000 horse power to twin screws.

Until the advent of the Second World War *Strathmore* maintained the Australia service. War was declared while she was on a Mediterranean cruise, her itinerary being changed to keep her in the Atlantic, arriving safely back on September 10th. During the war years, she was to serve her country as a troop ship, remaining unscathed throughout and finally being handed back to her owners in May 1948.

She was returned to her builders for reconditioning, making her first voyage back in commercial service to Australia on October 27th 1949.

In 1961 *Strathmore* was converted to carry 1,200 'tourist' class only, but this was only to be a shortlived reprieve from the inevitable, for on October 22nd 1963 her sale was announced, not to the breakers, but to Greek shipowner John S. Latsis, to be used for further trading. Handed over in Piraeus the following month, her name was changed to *Marianna Latsi* and then to *Henrietta Latsi* for Mecca pilgrim trade until 1969.

Orion
1935-1963

COMPLETED 1935	PASSENGERS	LENGTH 665 Feet
GROSS TONNAGE 23,371	486 First Class, 653 Tourist Class Crew 466	BEAM 82 Feet

Orion and her sister ship *Orcades* were built for the Orient Line by Vickers-Armstrong of Barrow in Furness. They were designed to be competition to the P&O 'Straths' and as such were to prove extremely popular ships, although *Orcades* was to have an all too brief career.

Unusually, *Orion* was launched by wireless on December 7th 1934, by the Duke of Gloucester who was the Governor General out in Australia. She was fitted with single reduction geared steam turbines producing 24,000 Indicated Horse Power to twin screws giving a maximum speed of twenty one knots. She was to make a shakedown cruise in September 1935, and during the voyage answered a distress call put out by the White Star liner *Doric*.

Orion's maiden voyage to Australia commenced on September 28th and she must have made a fine sight entering Sydney in the 'corn' livery Orient Line had adopted for their hulls. The first commercial years were brief, however, as she was requisitioned by the Government in September 1939, very soon after war with Germany was declared. She was converted to carry troops, with a new capacity of 5,449! *Orion* was to survive the conflict unscathed by enemy action, although she was unlucky enough to have a collision with *HMS Revenge* on September 15th 1941 during a convoy in the Indian Ocean. Fortunately damage was not severe and was soon repaired.

Handed back to her owners in 1946, *Orion* returned to Barrow to be refitted and made her first post war voyage back on the Australia run in February of the following year. In 1954 she made three trips to Vancouver and San Francisco. These were to inaugurate a transpacific service for the company and one which P&O were to initiate also.

After the merger between P&O and Orient Line, *Orion* was to be employed for the low fare 'tourist' service, having a capacity for 1,691 passengers. Finally the vessel was employed as a floating hotel at Hamburg, from where she went for scrap to Antwerp.

Orcades
1937-1942

COMPLETED 1937
GROSS TONNAGE 23,456

PASSENGERS
463 First Class, 605 Tourist Class
Crew 466

LENGTH 664 Feet
BEAM 82 Feet

O*rcades* was completed two years after her sister ship, *Orion*, by the same yard at Barrow in Furness. Mechanically she was exactly the same, but a few improvements were obviously made, the most notable being her taller funnel. She had been launched on December 1st 1936, completed the following July, with an initial voyage to the Mediterranean. Her official maiden voyage to Australia commenced on October 9th.

Converted for trooping duties for the Second World War, she was only to survive another few years. She was lost on October 10th 1942, within forty eight hours of the sinking of her older sister *Oronsay*. *Orcades* was struck by two torpedoes at 11.30 in the morning when 217 miles from Capetown, homeward bound. She carried over 1,000 troops,

civilians and crew. Although down by the head, the ship remained on an even keel and it was attempted to run her back to Capetown. However, a third torpedo struck at 11.40am and all but a skeleton crew of 55 were sent away in boats. One boat was overturned by the rough sea and its occupants were lost. The ship proceeded on its one remaining engine, at about five knots; because of damaged steering gear could only steam in a wide circle. At 2.30pm she was struck by three more torpedoes and abandoned only just in time. In all 48 lives were lost, the survivors being picked up by a small Polish vessel the *Narwik*. Captain Fox, Commander of *Orcades*, was awarded both the C.B.E., for courage and leadership, and the Committee of Lloyd's War Medal for Bravery at Sea.

Himalaya
1949-1974

COMPLETED 1949	PASSENGERS	LENGTH 709 Feet
GROSS TONNAGE 28,047	758 First Class, 401 Tourist Class	BEAM 90 Feet
	Crew 572	

Himalaya was to be the first ship of the P&O post war building programme, being built for the Australia run by Vickers-Armstrong at Barrow in Furness. She was launched on October 5th 1948 and delivered to the company on September 1st 1949. The main machinery was steam turbines geared down to twin screws, cruising speed being 22 knots. She was the first liner to be fitted with a desallination plant for producing fresh water, capable of producing up to 350 tons a day.

The maiden voyage was to commence on October 6th from Tilbury to Bombay and Australia, cutting the passage time to Sydney down to thirty days. Himalaya was to continue on this run, with additional periods of cruising. In 1953, she had the distinctive 'Thornycroft' funnel top added to reduce soot fall on the after deck.

On August 30th 1956, she suffered her most unfortunate incident. An explosion caused by a gas leak in the refrigeration plant resulted in the deaths of three of the ships company, thirteen others being injured, two of whom died later in hospital in Malta.

Stabilisers and air conditioning were fitted in 1959, and in 1963 she was converted to one class 'tourist', her capacity being increased to 1,416. From then on she was to operate cruises of varying duration. She was to be the last P&O passenger ship to call at Tilbury. From then on P&O liners were to use Southampton as their terminal port.

In May 1974 she left Southampton for the last time, cruising then out of Sydney for a few months, leaving there on October 19th for Hong Kong, and finally in November to the breakers yard in Taiwan.

Chusan
1950-1973

COMPLETED 1959
GROSS TONNAGE 24,215

PASSENGERS
474 First Class, 514 Tourist Class
Crew 572

LENGTH 672 Feet
BEAM 85 Feet

Chusan, the second vessel in the P&O post war replacement programme, was another product of the Vickers Barrow yard. She was launched on June 29th 1949. During the launch *Chusan* rolled alarmingly as a result of a broken launching cradle on the starboard bow, fortunately no damage was caused. Twelve months later she was handed over and commenced her career with a series of cruises, the maiden voyage to Madeira and Lisbon sailing on July 1st from Southampton.

Chusan had taken almost three and a half years to build, as a result the cost had risen to £3.25 million, a million pounds more than expected. Below, her main engines were geared turbines, four boilers developing 42,500 SHP to twin screws, giving her a cruising speed of 23 knots. She was the first large liner to have Denny-Brown stabilisers.

In September she sailed for Bombay and finally, on November 7th, she sailed for the Far East, the route for which she had been intended, although Japan was not added until 1952. In June of 1953 she had a collision in the English Channel with the cargo vessel *Prospector*, which resulted in a two day delay while the damaged bow was repaired.

She maintained this route until 1963, but also continued with cruises of varying duration, including a 92 day world cruise in 1959. From June 1963 she was placed on the Australia run and spent more time in the Pacific. However, along with other liners of the age, she was to suffer the unfair competition of the jet aircraft, plus the rising cost of fuel oil. She was withdrawn from service in March 1973, sailing finally on May 12th from Southampton to breakers in Taiwan.

Orsova
1954-1974

The *Orsova* of 1954 was the last vessel in a trio built by the Orient Line to replace lost and ageing tonnage after the Second World War. The first had been *Orcades* in 1948, followed by *Oronsay* in 1951. They were all built at the Vickers-Armstrong yard at Barrow in Furness, powered by double reduction geared steam turbines to twin shafts and designed for the Australian trade.

Orcades, at twenty two knots, was to herald a faster era to this service, bringing the passage time down from thirty six to twenty six days. The design of all three ships was an obvious continuation from that of the pre war *Orion*, with the bridge and funnel close together near the centre single mast over the wheelhouse, and the most characteristic of all being their 'Welsh Bonnet' on the funnel top.

Before *Oronsay* was handed over, in October of 1950, she had a serious fire in number two hold while at the fitting out yard. The blaze was contained, although holes had to be cut in the ships side to allow the water, being pumped in to extinguish the fire, to escape before the ship capsized. Even so, she was delivered seven months later in May 1951.

Orsova was launched on May 14th 1953. She was to be the Orient Lines penultimate passenger ship before the merger with P&O, and as such was the new company flagship, resplendent in the companies 'corn' livery. Her maiden voyage commenced on March 17th 1954, eastbound to Australia via the Suez Canal. During the passage, on April 5th, she passed the Shaw Savill liner *Gothic*, which was at that time being used as the Royal Yacht. Her Majesty Queen Elizabeth and The Duke of Edinburgh were on board, homeward bound from their coronation world tour, signals were exchanged and fireworks were ignited, no doubt thrilling the passengers as both ships passed quite close.

In the following year, *Orcades* initiated the service to Australia via the Panama Canal, calling at Bermuda, Port Everglades, Nassau, Kingston, the Canal, Los Angeles, San Francisco, Vancouver, Honolulu, Fiji, Auckland, Wellington, Sydney and Melbourne. *Orsova* went around the world in the same year, covering 46,000 miles and another first which has resulted in the company offering an annual world voyage ever since.

After the merger, the Orient Liners were repainted with white hulls and red boot-topping, the ships continued on the same routes with more cruising from the U.K. and Australia, but by the early seventies with the advent of the wide bodied airliner on all long distance routes, more and more trade was being lost. P&O placed their liners in every conceivable market place, but basically they were too big and there were too many for the up and coming cruise market. That, and the escalating price of crude oil, resulted in the disappearance of many large passenger vessels, Kaohsiung in Taiwan was to become their graveyard. The first of the big three to go was *Orcades*, sold in February 1973. *Orsova*, although not the oldest, was to follow in February 1974, having been laid up in Southampton since the previous November. *Oronsay* survived just a little longer, but inevitably she was to come under the breakers torch, finally being sold in Hong Kong and making the overnight run to Kaohsiung on October 6th 1975.

COMPLETED 1954
GROSS TONNAGE 28,790

PASSENGERS
694 First Class, 809 Tourist Class
Crew 620

LENGTH 723 Feet
BEAM 91 Feet

Arcadia & Iberia
1954-1979   1954-1972

GROSS TONNAGE 29,664 (29,614)

PASSENGERS
679 First Class, 735 Tourist Class
Crew 710

LENGTH 721 (719) Feet
BEAM 91 Feet

Arcadia and *Iberia* were the second pair of post-war passenger vessels ordered by P&O, the first from the John Brown yard on Clydebank and the latter from Harland and Wolff, Belfast. They were sister ships, yet looked distinctly different, due solely to the funnel design. The company were experimenting with different designs to ensure smoke and soot cleared the after decks. *Arcadia* was to have the rounded 'Clydebank' funnel, while *Iberia*'s was slightly more unconventional and partially hidden by the coaming.

Arcadia was the first to be launched on May 14th 1953, the *Iberia* on January 21st 1954. Both ships were designed for the Australia service and had identical machinery, geared steam turbines, developing 42,500 IHP to twin screws, giving a service speed of 22 knots.

Maiden voyages commenced on February 22nd and September 28th respectively, from London to Sydney via Bombay. *Arcadia* was to go to the Harland and Wolff yard in 1959 to have air conditioning fitted, after which she cruised in the Pacific, she

went on the trans-pacific service, and was to be employed more and more in the cruise market. She survived the transition from the liner service to cruising whereas many other vessels, including her sister, did not. From 1968 she cruised from US ports to the Carribbean, and after having her main mast removed and her foremast shortened in 1979, she was able to cruise Alaskan waters.

In May 1973, *Arcadia* was converted to a one class ship with a capacity for 1,350 passengers. She continued to cruise in various

locations around the world, making her last voyage out of the UK in 1976, after which she was permanently based in Sydney, replacing *Himalaya*. On January 29th 1979, she left Sydney for the last time, making a cruise up to Singapore, where the passengers were to leave and embark onto *Sea Princess*, P&O's latest acquisition. From Singapore she made her way to Kaohsiung in Taiwan to be broken up, having been bought by Nisshoi-Iwai Co of Japan.

Iberia had a slightly more chequered career, she was involved in a collision in 1956 with the tanker *Stanvan Pretoria* off Colombo, where temporary repairs had to be carried out. Permanent repairs were effected at Sydney and took eighteen days. A cruise out of Tilbury had to be cancelled as a result. She had an epidemic of gastro-enteritis in 1958 which necessitated twelve passengers being hospitalised. In 1961, she was modernised for cruising which also entailed the fitting of stabilisers. Like *Arcadia*, she was to be more engaged cruising, but by the late sixties her mechanical reliability was becoming uncertain. Electrical failures were not uncommon, the starboard engine failed in Acapulco and even the stabilisers were put out of action by a power failure during an Atlantic gale in December 1969.

When the company had to thin out their tonnage in the early seventies as a result of the rising fuel prices and the increase in passengers travelling by air, the *Iberia*, because of her poor reliability, must have been a logical first choice. She returned to Southampton from Sydney on April 19th 1972, and was laid up for two months awaiting disposal, finally leaving on June 28th, en route for breakers in Taiwan.

Oriana
1960-1986

Oriana was to be the last liner built for the Orient Line, and the last with the distinctive corn coloured hull. A great deal of information must have been exchanged between the company and P&O at the design stage, as they were both to come out with ships similar in performance and capacity if not in appearance. Oriana was the first, launched by Princess Alexandra on November 3rd 1959 from the Barrow yard of Vickers Armstrong. She was the largest passenger ship to have been built in England, and although in design she was a logical progression from the Orsova, she had a modern appearance characterised by a 'working' funnel and another 'vent' funnel further aft and lower down. Her machinery was the well proven steam turbines, which were double reduction geared to twin shafts and fed by four water tube boilers. A design speed of 27.5 knots had been asked for, but in fact during her trials in November 1960, she was to exceed 30 knots.

This speed was, of course, to make a considerable change to the schedule to Australia. After an initial shake-down cruise to Lisbon with the Association of British Travel Agents on board, her maiden voyage from Southampton to Sydney commenced on 3rd December. The passage time was reduced to three weeks, as a result of which Oriana was to be awarded the 'Golden Cockerel' for the fastest passage, a record she still holds.

Oriana and her P&O partner Canberra, which was to follow a year later, were to be the most successful liners on the route, however, success was to be relatively short lived. They continued the liner service to the west coast of America and then round the world via the Panama Canal back to England. By 1966 all the Orient liners had been transferred to P&O ownership, the corn coloured hull had gone, and P&O-Orient became just P&O. By the early seventies the liner service was becoming a luxury of the past, air travel having finally taken over the carriage of regular travellers to the Far East and Australasia. Consequently P&O were to place their ships more into the cruising trade, P&O Cruises being formed and all their passenger fleet put under this new banner.

Oriana was converted to become a one class 'tourist' ship with a capacity for 1,700 passengers and she went cruising permanently, mainly from the UK but after 1981 she replaced the Arcadia in the Australian cruise market. Even here she outlived her competitiveness and in March 1986 she was withdrawn, returning from her last Pacific cruise on the 27th. She left Sydney on 29th May, under tow, her destination Japan. She had been bought by Daiwa House Sales for use as a static hotel and convention centre in Beppu Bay on the island of Kyushu.

During her years with P&O, Oriana had passed through the Suez Canal thirty nine times and the Panama Canal fifty six times. Between the 25th and 26th of May 1963, whilst on passage betwen Suez and Aden, she covered a distance of 701 miles at an average speed of 29.21 knots, an unbroken record.

COMPLETED 1960
GROSS TONNAGE 41,923

PASSENGERS
638 First Class,
1,496 Tourist Class. Crew 790

LENGTH 804 Feet
BEAM 97 Feet

Chitral & Cathay
1961-1970

COMPLETED 1956 (1957)
GROSS TONNAGE 13,821 (13,531)

PASSENGERS
274 First Class
Crew 214

LENGTH 558 Feet
BEAM 70 Feet

These two delightful ships were not built for the P&O Line, but for CMB (Compagnie Maritime Belge) to run on the established cargo/passenger route between Antwerp and the Belgian Congo. *Jadotville*, which was to become *Chitral*, was built in France by SA des Chantiers et Ateliers of St Nazaire and completed in July 1956, while *Baudouinville (Cathay)* was built at Antwerp by Anon Cockerill-Ougree and came into service in November the following year. They were single screw steam turbine ships capable of 17 knots.

They would probably have remained on their run, however, the Congo became independent in June 1960, the result being that both vessels became surplus to their owners requirements. P&O purchased them to replace the ageing *Carthage* and *Corfu* on the Far East run. *Chitral* was the first, making her initial voyage for her new company from London on 28th February 1961. *Cathay* followed on April 14th. Both ships changed from the light grey hulls and yellow funnels of CMB to the white and buff of P&O, accommodation being altered to 235 passengers.

In 1967 the Suez Canal was closed as a result of the Middle East War, this necessitated both ships having to travel via the Cape, increasing the distance considerably. For this reason and the prominence of the wide-bodied aircraft in

long distance travel, trade for the two ships began to decline, *Chitral* experimented with cruising for a short time, but it was decided to withdraw both ships in late 1969. They were not sold but transferred to the P&O subsidiary, the Eastern and Australian Company Ltd. *Cathay* went over to Hong Kong in November 14th 1969 and *Chitral* followed on October 12th 1970. The ships, with their large freezer capacity, were ideal for the E&A route between Australia, the Far East and Japan.

Yet again the two ships were to suffer the consequences of progress, this time it was the increasing use of container cargoes which forced E&A to dispense with both vessels in late 1975. *Chitral* went to breakers in Taiwan, having been sold on December 3rd. *Cathay* was more fortunate. On January 28th 1976 she was sold to Red China for use as a cadet training ship and renamed *Kenghsin*, later to be renamed *Shanghai* and placed on the regular run between Hong Kong and Shanghai where, it is believed, she is still employed.

Canberra
1961-In Service

Canberra was totally different from any ship P&O had ordered before. Along with Orient Line's *Oriana*, she was planned for the three week service to Australia, but there was to be no other similarity between the two ships.

Ordered from the Belfast yard of Harland and Wolff, she was launched on March 16th 1960. The main machinery is turbo-electric, two steam turbines providing 82,500 IHP to two generators, which in turn provide power to two electric motors, these having been built by AEI at Rugby. Two propellers give a service speed of 27.5 knots, however, 29.27 knots was recorded on the trials in May 1961. It was in her design that she was to differ from all that had preceeded her, the machinery is aft which allows for more accommodation and deck space amidships and she has twin funnels aft, the bridge is forward of midships and her lifeboats are stowed three decks below the upper deck, underslung within the dimensions of the hull.

The maiden voyage from Southampton to Colombo, Melbourne and Sydney commenced on June 2nd 1961 and then continued on to the west coast of North America.

By the late sixties it became obvious as a result of the increase in long distance air travel, plus the spiralling cost of fuel oil, that the days of the liner service had gone. *Canberra* cruised the Caribbean from New York in early 1973, however, this was not a success and later that year the company offered her for sale. The decision was reversed some weeks later and in early 1974 she was converted

for one class cruising, her capacity being reduced to 1,737 passengers. She has maintained this role ever since, with cruises of varying duration from Sydney and Southampton, as well as completing a world cruise most years.

There has, however, been one major interuption to her routine. In April 1982, *Canberra* was requisitioned by the British Government to assist in the carriage of personnel during what is now referred to as the 'Falklands Conflict'. As part of the British 'Task Force' she was to leave Southampton on April 9th with troops from the 3rd Battalion, Parachute Regiment, 40 Commando and Royal Marines. Eventually, anchoring in San Carlos Water, she was disembarking her troops on May 21st, when she and the other ships came under intense attack

by the Argentine Air Force. She remained unscathed, even though her great size made her the obvious target and she sailed that night for South Georgia where she embarked more troops from the Cunard liner, *Queen Elizabeth 2*, which had also been requisitioned. *Canberra* returned to 'bomb alley', where fog fortunately covered the disembarkation. She returned to the cover of the South Atlantic until the Argentine occupying forces had surrendered, she was then used to carry over 5,000 prisoners to the Argentine port of Puerto Madryn, where she had been guaranteed safe passage. She was to return to Port Stanley to pick up British troops for the passage home and finally arrived in Southampton on July 11th to probably the most tremendous welcome a ship has ever had in British waters.

CANBERRA 44,807 grt
Cruise liner
P&O Passenger Division

COMPLETED 1961
GROSS TONNAGE 44,807

PASSENGERS
548 First Class
1,690 Tourist Class. Crew 803

LENGTH 819 Feet
BEAM 102 Feet

Postcard Miscellany

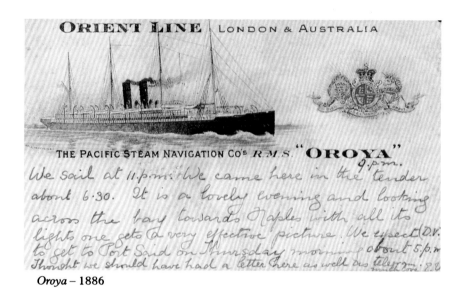

ORIENT LINE LONDON & AUSTRALIA

THE PACIFIC STEAM NAVIGATION CO's *R.M.S.* "OROYA"

9.p.m.

We sail at 11.p.m. We came here in the tender about 6.30. It is a lovely evening and looking across the bay towards Naples with all its lights one gets a very effective picture. We expect (D.V.) to get to Port Said on Thursday morning about 5.p.m. Thought we should have had a letter here as well as telegram.

with love. E.B.

Oroya – 1886

ORIENT-ROYAL MAIL LINE S.S. ORMUZ
ENTERING NAPLES.

Ormuz – 1886

Himalaya – 1892

Omrah – 1899

Plassy – 1899

Orontes – 1902

Macedonia – 1904

Osterley – 1909

Mantua – 1909

Bendigo – 1922